FriesenPress

Suite 300 - 990 Fort St
Victoria, BC, Canada, V8V 3K2
www.friesenpress.com

Copyright © 2015 by Murali Murthy.
First Edition — 2015

All rights reserved.

No part of this publication may be reproduced in any form, or by any means, electronic or mechanical, including photocopying, recording, or any information browsing, storage, or retrieval system, without permission in writing from FriesenPress.

ISBN
978-1-4602-7613-6 (Hardcover)
978-1-4602-7614-3 (Paperback)
978-1-4602-7615-0 (eBook)

1. *Self-Help*

Distributed to the trade by The Ingram Book Company.

"This is an astonishing and abundant world we live in; and there is way more than enough energy, material, ingenuity, creativity and ambition to allow every human being on the planet to succeed."

\- Robert Kiyosaki

DEDICATION

This book is dedicated to my sons, Ekaansh, 11, and Ayush, 6. And indeed to every young boy and girl around the world.

For their fearless spirit.

For understanding how to demand what they desire from the universe.

For living life with courage, resolution and limitless hope.

For their boundless imagination.

For viewing the world through a kaleidoscope of infinite possibilities.

For instinctively knowing how to live in the moment.

For their innocence and joy.

For their ability to forgive and give unconditional love.

For showing us all how to live a life of Abundance.

Truly, as William Wordsworth wrote: "The child is father of the man".

TABLE OF CONTENTS

Dedication   v

Acknowledgements   ix

Praise for The ACE Abundance   xi

Foreword   xvii

Introduction   xix

How to Make the Most of This Book   xxiii

CHAPTER 1   1
An Abundance of OPTIMISM

CHAPTER 2   13
An Abundance of OPPORTUNITY

CHAPTER 3   25
An Abundance of INITIATIVE

CHAPTER 4   37
An Abundance of PASSION

CHAPTER 5   49
An Abundance of ACTIVITY

CHAPTER 6   63
An Abundance of VALUE

CHAPTER 7   77
An Abundance of TRUST

CHAPTER 8   89
An Abundance of KINDNESS

CHAPTER 9   101
An Abundance of GRATITUDE

CHAPTER 10   113
An Abundance of COURAGE

CHAPTER 11   127
An Abundance of INTEGRITY

CHAPTER 12   139
An Abundance of SELF-ESTEEM

Bonus   153

Abundance Affirmations   157

References   159

Other Books in The ACE Series   163

ACKNOWLEDGEMENTS

How can you write a book on how to attract Abundance? It's simple. Just surround yourself with people who have an Abundance Mentality.

The last two years have been filled with magnificent "Abundance" which has flowed into my life in many ways. And I am brimming with gratitude for each one of the Abundance Minded People [AMP] who made the fulfilling effort of writing this special book possible.

Thank you

To my beautiful wife Shalu for always being there and providing invaluable suggestions on everything from the cover image selection to the font size and content quality on each page.

To my sister Jaya Ashok, for constantly stretching me and being my most vociferous advocate.

To Myrna Riback, my iron-fisted editor, who has been virtually working as hard as I have on this project. Myrna and I have collaborated on all three ACE books and I cannot imagine how I could have finished this one if it were not for her constant faith in The ACE series. Thank you, Myrna. This work is truly also yours!

To Girish Mehta and his entire team at Adventure Global, Dubai - Nilesh, Siju and Vaisakh. They all deserve recognition for devoting their invaluable time and for their deft design skills which resulted in making this book a breezy read.

To everyone in the *Crown Eagles 1000 Family* who inspire me daily to reach for my dreams and to aim for the stars.

To the Friesen Press team for their smooth production process and faith in my expanding list of projects and enterprises. This is my third collaboration with them and their help, as always, has been invaluable.

Last, but not the least, I want to acknowledge my loyal readers who have been with me from the start. Thank you all for providing me with the reason to write and share. Your unflagging support has helped me face many challenges over the years and to become a better writer. It is wonderful to know that I have been able to bring you books that you can enjoy as much as I have enjoyed writing them.

You are the true ACE.

Murali Murthy

PRAISE FOR *THE ACE ABUNDANCE*

"Murali lays out a very practical approach to a topic that in the past has been labeled inspirational and spiritual. So for those of you who are thinking this is another one of those 1990's "Abundance movement" concepts, you could not be more wrong.

This book does not try to sell you on the idea that you need to have faith in the path the author is leading you. Instead, it actually connects treating people well, and making them feel valued, to the inevitable result of not needing to compete with others for resources. So you don't know that you have been spiritually inspired until about an hour after you've read the book.

Murali writes with Guru-ish feel that can be very dramatic and direct at times *(Deepak Chopra meets Ernest Hemingway)* but that actually makes it a fun read easily devoured on a plane ride from Chicago to L.A. Murali is a great writer overall and this is a very good book that is by far the best of its genre."

- Garrison Wynn, CSP, CEO, Wynn Solutions, Bestselling Author, *The Real Truth About Success and The Cowbell Principle,* Speaker and Consultant, www.garrisonwynn.com, www.wynnsolutions.com.

"Murali's latest book empowers you with an unshakable, clear understanding of the Abundance principles and lets you apply them right away. If you take all the concepts outlined in *The ACE Abundance* and condense them into simple daily practices, you will be able to create your own destiny and keep expanding your Abundance throughout your life."

- Patrick Snow, International Best-Selling Author of *Creating Your Own Destiny*, *The Affluent Entrepreneur*, and *Boy Entrepreneur*, Professional Keynote Speaker, Publishing and Book Marketing Coach, Speaking Coach. www.PatrickSnow.com, www.ThePublishingDoctor.com

"The world around us is constantly bombarding us with various thoughts and happenings. Much of which, if we are not careful will leave us with a feeling of desperation and fear that nothing good ever happens. Of course this isn't the case. Far from it actually. In fact, there is much prosperity and Abundance going on all around us, yes, even in our own life if we would only allow ourselves to see it. Murali Murthy does a wonderful job of teaching the skills necessary to see and unleash an abundant, more fulfilling life in his book *The ACE Abundance*. He pulls together a combination of very inspiring stories which builds on each chapter and lesson in the book. At the same time he gives you practical steps you can take in order to develop the necessary skills for an abundant mindset. You're going to enjoy this inspiring and encouraging book."

- Josh Hinds, Speaker, Entrepreneur, Founder of GetMotivation.com and Author of *It's Your Life, LIVE BIG*

"*The ACE Abundance* is a marvelous compilation of meaningful stories, quick tips and reminders of how to live our best life. Each of the 12 chapters hits on one area of our inner landscape to develop and nurture. It offers both new ideas to consider, reminders of what we already know and often forget, and "bite size" action steps to take that can lead to big outcomes. I really like the repeating structure in each chapter that keeps my short attention span in check and interested to continue reading. I have already printed out the bonus pages with 12 tips to excel as an Abundance Minded Person - or AMP as Murali calls us, and the Abundance affirmations. I really enjoyed reading this book and will review it from time to time when I need to reconnect with my abundant self."

- Barbara Rogoski, Executive Speaker Coach, TEDx Speaker Coach and Author of *Boring to Brilliant! A Speaker's Guide,* **www.Successfulspeakernow.com**

"Once again, Murali Murthy has demonstrated his unique ability to deliver clear and actionable steps for personal growth. In *The ACE Abundance*, he takes the philosophy of Abundance thinking to a whole new level by wrapping it in his powerful, practical, action-oriented ACE framework. A must read for all!"

- Andrew Srinarayan, Vice President, WelcomePack Canada Inc., **www.WelcomePackCanada.com**

"*The ACE Abundance* starts with the premise that we are inhibited in many aspects of our lives by a mentality of scarcity. It then provides a simple and step-by-step guide to overcoming this mentality and fostering a mentality of Abundance and the positive improvements that come with that. It illustrates each step by an eclectic range of examples. It is the kind of book that you can keep and constantly turn to inspire you in a variety of personal objectives."

- Robin Brown, Co-Author, *Migration Nation: A Practical Guide to Doing* *Business in Globalized Canada* **and Group VP - Cultural Markets & Consumer** **Insights, www.environics.ca**

"I love this book! You can choose to be "bitter or better" is such a powerful statement because many things we accept as fate or circumstance is in reality a choice we make or made. Everything positive truly starts from optimism and *The ACE Abundance* is

Praise for *The ACE Abundance*

overflowing with it. In fact, I would rather call this book a manual, because it really should be essential reading for anybody over the age of 16. Call it a refresher course or book of life, I hope everyone in the world not only reads *The ACE Abundance* but puts in practice the principles behind it."

- Marcus Paul, President, Blixitt Inc., www.Blixitt.com

"To ACE life and live in Abundance, read and savour this inspiring book. ACE stands for **Absorb, Comprehend and Excel.** Each of the 12 chapters highlights another aspect of Abundance in our lives. We have all we need if only we opened up our eyes, minds and hearts to it. Buy a copy for everyone you know. They will thank you for it."

- Patti Pokorchak, MBA, Entrepreneur, Speaker, Success Coach, Biz Sales Coach Author of *The Accidental Farmer: From Laptop to Llama and Back Again!*, www.SmallBizSalesCoach.ca

"*The ACE Abundance* Book is a follow up from Murali's already incredibly inspiring *The ACE Principle*. A step-by-step guide in how to live life abundantly, this book gives readers so much more than a recipe for success. Combining heartwarming and inspirational anecdotes from famous and not so famous people from all walks of life, Murali effectively leaves readers with a complete experience for how to live better. A highly recommended read for anyone looking to get into business, grow their business, improve their life, or simply learn to appreciate all that they have."

- Nadine Evans, CEO, Canadian Association of Marketing Professionals, www.Canadianmarketer.ca

"*The ACE Abundance* is a powerful reminder of the infinite possibilities that lie within us. This brilliant must-read book is the perfect antidote to scarcity-thinking and provides the key to creating the happiness that we so desperately seek.

Through vivid examples and anecdotes in 12 breezy chapters, Murali reminds us that our choices always come from within and we can choose, right now, to think positive and create an abundantly rich life."

- Josh Linkner, Tech Entrepreneur, Hyper-Growth Leader, Keynote Speaker, and Two-time NY Times Bestselling Author, *Disciplined Dreaming and The Road to Reinvention,* www.JoshLinkner.com

"In *The ACE Abundance*, Murali reveals how to tap into your passion and purpose to create Abundance. This book will help you go from limitations to limitless possibilities. If you can suspend your judgment for just one moment to read it, you will experience a shift in your current thinking."

- Rene Godefroy, Best-Selling Author of *Kick Your Excuses Goodbye,* Motivational Speaker, Humanitarian, www.ReneGodefroy.com

"If you want to live a happier, healthier more abundant life, then this book is for you! Murali Murthy does an incredible job of showing you how to master the 12 key traits that will enable you to live the life you were born to live... a life of true Abundance!"

- Michelle Prince, Best-Selling Author, Zig Ziglar Motivational Speaker & Self-Publishing Expert, www.MichellePrince.com

"*The ACE Abundance* opens the world's eyes, once again, to the power of basic human truths. You must take responsibility for your life, create your destiny, seek mutual benefit, understand and serve others, but most of all be abundant to gain Abundance. When we do so, we not only change our own lives, but we change the world. The 12 principles outlined in this book are not only essential to your well being, but are a vital part of achieving anything you desire in Abundance.

The ACE Abundance contains the kind of penetrating truth about human nature and the Abundance that is available around us, that one has to pause and think. It will not only light a fire within you and inspire you to daily action, but will keep you moving forward towards achieving the Abundance you truly deserve. Murali elucidates that to excel beyond expectations requires us to tap into our own physical, mental and spiritual resources, and this is exactly what we need this very moment."

- Lincoln Holnes, Acclaimed Sales Coach, Trainer, Speaker,
www.hanhconsulting.com

"Murali Murthy's *The ACE Abundance: 12 Amazing Ways to Live an Abundant Life Everyday* is a book for everyone who believes they can have more: more opportunity, more value, more passion, more LIFE.

More importantly, it's a book for everyone who doesn't believe they can have more."

- Barry Maher, Keynote Speaker, Workshop Leader and Author of *Filling the Glass: The Skeptic's Guide to Positive Thinking in Business*, www.barrymaher.com

"Murali Murthy is an energetic and inspiring leader who shares his secrets in *The ACE Abundance*.

His ACE format makes each concept easy to understand and apply in your life. Read this book to discover simple yet powerful strategies to create greater Abundance in your life."

- Wendy Woods, Principal, Watershed Training Solutions,
www.watershedtraining.ca

FOREWORD

They are right there. Just waiting for you. The real question is - are you ready for them?

Abundance, resources, and a world of possibilities – they're all yours. They're merely waiting to be discovered.

And as we coach hundreds of executives and leaders all over the world, we find so many who are afraid of not having enough. Not having enough time. Not having enough money. Not having enough influence. Not having enough vision.

So to compensate for the lack of resources, they search relentlessly for new opportunities, more resources, and greater influence. Only to be disappointed.

And although there's nothing inherently wrong with searching and asking for help, I've learned that leaders who give freely of themselves, seeking nothing in return, never seem to need anything. The more people think they need from others, the more they seem to lack.

What if the secret to Abundance isn't found in searching for what you lack and manipulating the universe into giving it to you. What if the secret to Abundance is in observing and appreciating what's

xvii

right in front of you and making the most of the relationships and resources that are already yours.

No matter what you're looking for – greater efficiency and effectiveness, higher revenue or income, to lead better through change, to develop leadership skills – you are surrounded by Abundance. What you need is available every time you need it.

Murali Murthy is the author of one of the most important books you'll ever read – *The ACE Abundance*. It will get you moving when you're stuck. It will give you what you need to dig out of the hole you've created. It will kick you in the seat of the pants when you need it.

If you haven't already bought it, this is your chance. Maybe your only chance. Your last chance – to change the rest of your life, your career, your legacy.

Extraordinary belongs to those who proactively become it. And Abundance belongs to those who ardently use it.

In one of the most encouraging books I've ever read, Murali gets real practical, direct, and personal. Read it fast – then read it again and make notes. Develop a SIMPLE plan and take action.

Then buy a copy for everyone else who's stuck and help them get moving.

Are you ready to be amazed at what's possible in your life and work?

Dr. Michael Nichols
Founder of *Guidestone University* and *The Retreat at*
Guidestone Hills
Author of *Creating Your Business Vision*
www.michaelnichols.org

INTRODUCTION

You were born to
Absorb, Comprehend and Excel
in Abundance.

Free yourself from the crippling belief of scarcity.

Many in society seem to be weighed down by a scarcity mentality. This is a belief that convinces people there is a lack of everything in life, including opportunity. To believe that life can never offer more, causes a painful and unfulfilling existence for many and creates a great deal of unnecessary fear, anxiety and desperation.

On the other hand, a mentality that fosters the belief in Abundance, allows people to believe that there are always new chances and opportunities to do better. This positive view allows one to see life in a long-term perspective rather than as a series of debilitating disappointments.

Believing that Abundance is not only possible but probable can help improve a person's performance and future prospects.

What do you see when you wake up every morning?

Do you see a gloomy day with nothing but failure and disappointment ahead? Or do you wake up every morning and see the sky, the sun shining or the rain helping life around you grow. Do you feel the warmth of the benevolent universe?

Take a closer look at the world we live in. Look at all that it provided for us at no cost.

Just think how essential the air really is for the survival of our species, for all life. It exists for all who need it, for everything that lives on our planet. It expects nothing in return and yet we owe our lives to it. This is all the proof you need of unconditional love.

When you look at anything in nature, it is clear that Abundance is unlimited and scarcity does not actually exist except in our minds. In fact, the whole universe operates on the principle of enlargement and the creation of many from one.

We have simply been conditioned to believe in limited resources and scarcity. The concept of scarcity simply implies that the prices of goods, services and resources can go up over time and benefit those who control the supply.

The idea of Abundance and scarcity is much more than just an abstract concept. It very tangibly affects how we approach life. Those who believe strongly in scarcity tend to become cynical, fearful and guarded. But those who believe in Abundance tend to be aware, open, sharing and loving.

It is truly time for us to learn to recognize Abundance in the world around us. We must learn to tap into our own inner reserves that play their own part in creating Abundance of the universe.

How can we set Abundance in motion?

If we understand that our life's circumstances inevitably inspire a desire within us for Abundance, then we can also understand that those same circumstances can help us bring our desires into reality. We are not here to compete for the resources of the earth. It is truly liberating when we realize that the shortage is always, without exception, self-inflicted.

Once we realize and understand that we are not in competition with others who share our planet, that they cannot deprive us of something by taking it for themselves, we are truly free to pursue our dreams to their fulfillment. In fact, the existence of other people pursuing their dreams only enhances our ability to receive, to interact with others who have inspired our own desires. Our feeling of competition or shortage, of limitation of resources, only signals our misalignment with the universe, our inability to believe in our own desires and, ultimately, our ability to bring those desires to fruition.

Myth:

There is a finite container of resources that we are all dipping into with our requests. Therefore, when we satisfy our request for something, we automatically deprive others of that resource.

Reality:

All of the Abundance, resources and possibilities already exist. They are merely waiting to be discovered. When you hear or read about the 'creation' of Abundance or resources or solutions, understand that it is actually the 'discovery' of already existing Abundance, resources, and solutions.

When you desire an improvement to your life — your request for that improvement sends forth a signal and puts in motion a process of attraction and actualization of that improvement. In living abundant lives, we are merrily discovering and creating improved benefits.

You can make your every desire come true when you truly understand the ever-evolving, ever-expanding, ever-recreating pool of resources that already exists. When you understand that - the creative process of our planet - then you understand you have an important role to play in that expansion.

Start today.

A worldview of Abundance reminds you of the limitless nature of the universe and the self.

It instills trust and wonder and helps you connect more deeply to yourself, the world around you and other people.

It makes you open to sharing your modus operandi instead of competing for it.

It changes everything.

Go ahead, claim your Abundance.

HOW TO MAKE THE MOST OF THIS BOOK

Have you ever bought books on success principles?

If you have read or listened to any of these wonderful books and then simply moved on to the next one, you will agree that nothing in your life can change unless you actually put the techniques you learned into practice.

Similarly, it is not enough to read a book on attracting Abundance or cover the intellectual part about Abundance without understanding how to apply each concept to the changes your life requires.

The ACE Abundance includes powerful, targeted exercises and techniques and then helps you apply these techniques in hands-on, deliberate lessons. By applying these lessons to your own situation, you will be in a position to put each ACE concept into practice. Best of all . . . the techniques you will learn in this book take only minutes to apply.

Each chapter in this book will help you focus on three key areas:

1. As you **Absorb** every concept, each one will be comprehensively elucidated through a relevant, true story.

2. As you **Comprehend** the intellectual concepts, each one will be illuminated as to how and why it is important.

3. Finally, the hands-on, daily application of each concept in your life will show you how you can **Excel**.

Now you can ACE your life. A new life of ABUNDANCE awaits you!

Chapter 1 – An Abundance of Optimism

How you see the world and how you respond to changes will determine what you will eventually accomplish. Learn how an optimistic shift in attitude can lead to a strong, confident, happy person. And help you attract opportunity, success, love and - in short – an Abundance of everything the heart desires.

Chapter 2 – An Abundance of Opportunity

Learn how to establish the broader conditions for an Abundance mindset, by opening yourself up to a multitude of opportunities. Opportunities create an Abundance of potential; an Abundance of initiative, and an Abundance of creativity — which together reinforce the Abundance mindset.

Chapter 3 – An Abundance of Initiative

Your thoughts are powerful. Learn how you can harness this power and direct it exactly where you want it to go so you can improve any area of your life. By using your imagination to create a new story for your life, you can actually change the narrative.

Chapter 4 – An Abundance of Passion

There are actually endless ways that you can generate passion in your life. Learn how to start creating more and more 'gateways of passion' so that Abundance can flow more easily to you.

Chapter 5 – An Abundance of Activity

Living with purpose is one of the most powerful sources of Abundance you can generate in your life. Strip away all of the ignorance and confusion in living and discover how to bring purpose to your life. When you begin living with purpose, you will soon discover that an Abundance of activity and productivity will follow.

Chapter 6 – An Abundance of Value

Learn how to WOW people by constantly creating and giving value. Give off yourself abundantly, network authentically, share inspiring content, ideas and thoughts. And build deeper connections and relationships.

Chapter 7 – An Abundance of Trust

Trust is the major component in the foundation of successful interpersonal relationships. When people trust you, they're much more likely to believe in you and connect with you. Learn how to unleash limitless opportunities to attract and transfer trust.

Chapter 8 – An Abundance of Kindness

Acts of kindness make us feel valuable and alive. Unlock the doors to Abundance with a conscious effort to be even kinder by practicing kindness regularly. Learn how to spread the goodness and make a difference that has a lasting, ripple effect by simply asking "How can I create a little happiness for someone?"

Chapter 9 – An Abundance of Gratitude

Gratitude and Abundance are intricately intertwined; one cannot exist without the other. Allow yourself to see the world in a way that absorbs the goodness of humanity. Discover how you can use the positive traits of gratitude as a powerful tool to allow more Abundance into your life.

Chapter 10 – An Abundance of Courage

Being bold about what you believe in, will eventually shape what you achieve. Being courageous gives you the permission to dream bigger, unravel opportunities, imagine multiple potential ways, find the creative resources to do so and build the future you see.

Chapter 11 – An Abundance of Integrity

Live your life purposefully, with integrity and you will be motivated to do more, and then find outlets that let you grow professionally and personally. Adopting an authentic attitude is one of the most rewarding things you can do for yourself.

Chapter 12 – An Abundance of Self-esteem

Feeling worthy is the first step to opening yourself to Abundance. Learn how to develop the courage to develop a true, deep sense of worthiness. Believing in your own worthiness empowers you to make strong decisions that will result in Abundance.

CHAPTER 1
An Abundance of OPTIMISM

Absorb: Grasp the essence and the message behind the story.

Comprehend: Ask yourself how the message can apply to your life, career and relationships.

Excel: Take action. Put the insight to work.

Absorb The Optimism

The optimism of Kelsey Serwa

"I believe we are not shaped as individuals by the things that happen in our lives; we are shaped by the way we choose to deal with adversities, whether that be overcoming them or letting them overcome us."

- Kelsey Serwa

Kelsey Serwa is a Canadian freestyle skier and a member of the Canadian National Ski Cross Team. During the 2010-11 season, Serwa established herself as one of her sport's elite competitors, winning a bronze medal at the 2010 X Games and gold at the FIS World Championships Winter X Games. During those games, she had crashed through the finish line and injured her back just four days earlier but still stood atop the podium to collect her gold medal.

But Serwa encountered more adversity in January 2012. She had been leading the World Cup Ski Cross standing all season and the final heat of the day would settle who would land a spot on the Alpe D'Huez World Cup Podium in France. In that run, she went off a jump in a flat spin 360, missed the landing zone completely and tore the anterior crucial ligament in her left knee.

Kelsey had already had two knee surgeries but it wasn't until she went in for an MRI that she discovered some signs of arthritic growth in her knee joint. The biggest shock was how fast she had gone from being the best in the world to being knocked down to ground zero. Not only was she in great physically pain but also much mental distress.

She knew the road to recovery wasn't going to be easy but she was up to the task. In her own words, "Knowing this was going to

An Abundance of Optimism   5

be challenging gave me more motivation to work through it and push harder to come out positively on the other end".

Serwa was determined to do whatever she could to speed the healing. In early December, she was able to return to competition for the 2012-13 season's opening of the World Cup in Nakiska, Alberta. Then, two days before Christmas, she returned to the top of the podium, winning the World Cup on one of her favourite hills in San Candido, Italy.

By the time the Sochi Olympics came along in 2014, she had come back from several serious injuries and mental blocks to stand on the Olympic podium where she won silver behind teammate Marielle Thompson for Canada's record third 1-2 finish of the Games.

Comprehend the Optimism

Tap into the wellspring of positivity within.

Adverse experiences can leave us angry, confused and depressed. They are guaranteed to change us either by breeding self-doubt or by building resilience. It is our response to adversity that counts. It's up to us whether it makes us bitter or better.

Positivity starts from the inside and radiates to the outside. By understanding ourselves, we can increase our positivity.

Let your challenges develop maturity rather than drain your hope. Respond creatively to every adversity. Find the benefits of difficulties instead of reacting to them negatively.

> **Change your attitude, change your life.**
> **Learn how to get it,**
> **how to keep it**
> **and how to get it back if you lose it.**

Optimism helps you realize your true potential.

An Abundance of positivity allows us to aim for higher goals without the fear of failure. This mindset not only keeps us focused but more often allows us to attain our goals because we know it is possible and that it can be done. The positive outlook is the core motivation for us to keep trying and to eventually succeed.

Optimism and peace go hand in hand.

Peace is the reflection of inner optimism. When you are positive, you are calmer and more in control. This positivity will guide you

An Abundance of Optimism

and direct you. Nothing gives one person as much advantage as remaining cool and unruffled under turbulent circumstances.

Excel Through Optimism

1. See optimism as a choice.

Start by evaluating yourself and the people you meet. Everyone has a natural bent toward either cheerfulness or melancholy but anyone can choose optimism.

How do you relate to others? What is your attitude toward what you do? Is it positive or negative?

Optimism will not automatically change the reality of your situation. But it will change your attitude and outlook.

> **Optimism will give you a predisposition to activity.**
> **To look for,**
> **believe in**
> **and anticipate the best possible**
> **outcome in every situation.**

2. Immerse yourself in positivity.

Surround yourself with positive people. When adversity strikes, don't try to negotiate the pain on your own. Have people around you who can anchor you during life's storms.

In a growth environment, the accomplishments of those around you will encourage and challenge you to do more than you thought you could.

3. See adversity as a way to learn life lessons.

The potential for greatness lives within each of us and each of us is designed to do something great.

But there are many variables that affect our ability to succeed in life.

The choices we make can have good or bad consequences. If we make those choices out of positivity and peace – they will take us farther than those we make out of negativity and fear.

The choice you make, makes you. Don't dwell on your bad choices of the past. The good news is that every day holds new opportunity.

4. Safety in numbers.

You can have a more meaningful and fulfilling life. But you can't get there alone.

Don't drift through life – anchor it with a personal plan and a leadership coach who holds you accountable.

Build positive momentum through a structured growth plan.

Your Abundant Moment of **Optimism**

Unlock the limiting beliefs surrounding any one area in your life.

It could be the relationship with a loved one, career progress or job opportunities, issues regarding your health or money or any other life issue.

Write down the actual outcome you desire and read it out loud for a minimum of 21 days in a row.

You'll not only see your mind shifting from doubt to believing it is possible but this action alone could enable you to put into place a plan of action that takes you closer to the goal.

Absorb: Grasp the essence and the message behind the story.

Comprehend : Ask yourself how the message can apply to your life, career and relationships.

Excel: Take action. Put the insight to work.

Absorb the Opportunity

"The people who get on in this world are the people who get up and look for the circumstances they want and, if they can't find them, they make them."

- George Bernard Shaw

George de Mestral
The accidental innovator who seized his big opportunity.

Swiss engineer George de Mestral liked to walk his dog through the woods. When he did, he and his dog returned home covered in cockleburs and it took him a long while to disentangle them all.

De Mestral was impressed by how easily the burs latched on to his pants and the dog's fur and examined the burs under a microscope. He noted that the burs had numerous, miniscule hooks that enabled them to grasp hair or clothing.

What if, he wondered, he could find a way to make one material that was covered in tiny hooks, like the burs, and attach it to another material composed of small loops like the woven fabric of his trousers or dog fur? The two strips of synthetic material could then serve as a fastener like a zipper.

De Mestral felt the idea had merit and he took initiative to create a prototype in the hopes of patenting it. Friends warned him the project was foolhardy and would lead nowhere but he pressed on, undaunted by their skepticism.

To turn his idea into a commercial success, however, De Mestral had to figure out a way to manufacture the materials for his fastener inexpensively. Though his initial attempts at mass

An Abundance of Opportunity   **17**

production failed, he remained committed to the achievability of his idea.

De Mestral visited one weaver after another to try to convince one of them to make a prototype. At first, no one took him seriously. Eventually, through sheer stubbornness and persistence, he managed to persuade one weaver to take on the project. The idea was simple enough - hooks on one end, loops on the other - but try as he might, he couldn't find a material strong enough for the hooks.

After years of trial and error, De Mestral settled on nylon (a recent invention) as his material of choice. Although nylon, as strong as it was, seemed like the perfect material for the hooks, there was no known manufacturing process that could automate the production.

After a 20-year struggle, De Mestral received the patent for his invention: Velcro®

But it wasn't until NASA decided to use Velcro as fasteners for spacesuits that the orders started coming in. Then, some smart sporting goods designers saw how the same idea could be applied to ski apparel. From there, the invention took off.

Once people started to see other applications for the adhesive, it wasn't too long before Velcro made its way into wallets and sneakers. Today it's used in everything from child-safe dartboards to the cuffs in blood pressure meters.

Comprehend the Opportunity

Invest in persistence abundantly.

Many good ideas die because people give up easily. Even though you may have genius, passion and drive, you also need an Abundance of tenacity.

Even a very unusual idea can be wildly successful if you invest in persistence abundantly.

Seize the opportunities.

Windows of opportunity sometimes only stay open for a few, brief moments. Hesitate, procrastinate, and the window closes shut. Grabbing hold of an opportunity before it's gone is key.

**An Abundance mentality is not luck.
Successful people hunt opportunity down,
make sacrifices
and work hard.**

Abundance mentality and patience lead to success and more opportunity.

An Abundance mentality holds that there is enough of everything for everybody. And patience is the starting point for building Abundance in your life.

An Abundance of Opportunity

Excel with Opportunity

1: Believe you deserve it.

Once you accept the idea that Abundance of everything exists on this planet, believe that you are worthy of receiving unlimited opportunities. Why wait for opportunity to knock on the door when you can keep the door open to welcome it in?

2: Change your outlook.

The successful person lives in a world of abundant opportunities.
Develop an attitude of hopeful confidence
and you will begin to view the world
as a reservoir of endless opportunity.

3: Opportunity is literally everywhere.

Be keen, observant and open to receive opportunity. You too could literally stumble upon it the next time you take a walk.

4: Challenges lead to new opportunities.

Look at your problems and challenges closely. Don't view them as setbacks. Sometimes the solution is hidden within the challenge. Birds and airplanes fly by constantly engaging in a tug of war between the opposing forces of lift versus weight; thrust versus drag.

An Abundance of Opportunity

5: Create your new sphere of opportunity.

Make a conscious decision to associate with Abundance Minded People [AMP] more often. Read innovation and development blogs, listen to success stories and watch personal development material.

Your Abundant Moment of **Opportunity**

Share your best ideas. Opportunity breeds opportunity.

Think of the PC revolution a few decades back and the social media revolution now. Think of the smart phone revolution of a few years back and look at the onslaught of Apps right now. Opportunity truly breeds greater opportunity.

If you believe you are on to the next big thing, and even if it is just a kernel of an idea, share it with your AMPs.

Work out a plan to see it through to its fruition.

Who knows what possibilities and opportunities you could unearth in a few days, months or years from now?

Absorb: Grasp the essence and the message behind the story.

Comprehend: Ask yourself how the message can apply to your life, career and relationships.

Excel: Take action. Put the insight to work.

Absorb the Initiative

"You have not lived today until you have done something for someone who can never repay you."

- John Bunyan

Adam Braun, a man who took the initiative. Founder and CEO of Pencils of Promise.

Pencils of Promise [PoP] is an award-winning, non-profit organization that has built schools across Africa, Asia and Latin America for children in poverty.

While traveling as a college student, Braun met a young boy begging on the streets in India. When he asked him what he would want if he could have anything in the world, the boy's answer was simply, "a pencil." That answer changed Braun's life and he became obsessed with bringing top-notch business acumen into the humanitarian sector.

He started working with hedge funds at Bain and Company when he was 16 years old and learned early that results speak louder than anything else. On Wall Street, you are held accountable by your performance and that forces you to make decisions based on perceived value rather than emotion.

In October 2008, Braun went to his local bank and deposited $25 in hopes of building one school in the developing world. Under his stewardship which blends non-profit idealism with for-profit business principles, the organization managed to deliver over 10 million educational hours to children in poverty on four continents - all within four years of its launch.

Born in one of the worst economic conditions possible, PoP forced Braun to create an innovative approach to fundraising and he developed the concept of asking kids to forgo birthday presents and asking their friends for donations instead. That strategy has since allowed his team to raise millions of dollars, break ground on more than 200 schools around the world and bring quality education to more than 20,000 children.

In addition, Braun was named to Forbes 30 Under 30 List in 2012.

On the organization's website, they state that "Pencils of Promise wants to test the edge of the world by feeling its curves... to see more, be more, do more... We know that we can create a better world through education."

Adam Braun echoes this philosophy in his book, *The Promise of a Pencil: How an Ordinary Person Can Create Extraordinary Change.*

In it, he explains the essential steps that every person must take to discover their own life of passion and purpose. *"Make your life a story worth telling. You only get one shot at this existence and, one day when you're gone, the most important thing you'll leave behind is the legacy of the life you lived. Make sure you make it a story you're proud to have others tell."*

Comprehend the Initiative

Abundance Minded People [AMP] understand that in order to go farther, they need to focus first on the advancement of others. Taking initiative can make a substantial difference – sometimes in one person's life and sometimes on the entire world.

The benefits of taking initiative:
a. Initiative builds momentum.

Abundance Minded People don't wait for guarantees before moving forward. They press ahead in spite of risks and build upon their successes gradually.

b. Initiative kills fear.

More people abandon their dreams out of fear than any other reason. But when you take the first step and start moving forward, you generate confidence to tackle the problems and obstacles in your path.

c. Initiative puts you out in front.

When people hesitate until they are forced to act through circumstances, they lose the advantage.

Initiative ensures you do the right thing
immediately upon realizing the best course of
action.
By proactively taking action,
you gain an edge on the competition.

An Abundance of Initiative

d. Initiative is rewarding.

Everyone has areas of strength in which they intuitively sense what needs to be done. Only those who marry intuition with action find the success they dream of.

Excel through Initiative

1. Find a cause you believe in.

Find something that moves you: an issue that inspires you or a creative solution to a problem. Then proceed to harness the fire that inspires you to make it happen.

2. Put the spotlight on others.

One of the best ways to help others is to do something for them that they cannot do for themselves.

> **When you focus your talents and abilities to help others,**
>> **you shine the brightest.**
>>> **Not only will that empower them,**
>>>> **it will give you personal fulfillment.**

3. Open more doors.

Learn how to connect people of like-minded goals and desires. Build networks and help build lives. Empower others by helping them connect with other people who might also be able help them.

4. Offer more opportunities.

When you place opportunities within reach of other people, it not only gives them a leg up to reach their goals, it empowers you by making you feel worthwhile and generous.

An Abundance of Initiative

5. Pass on your wisdom.

Perhaps the most precious resource Abundance Minded People can share is the wisdom gained through past experience. Be a mentor and find great gratification.

6. Give of yourself abundantly.

Harness your own resources to the best qualities of the people around you. In that way you become a prolific producer – both in achieving your own final goal and in helping those around them achieve success as well.

7. Give every situation your best.

Venturing into the unknown is frightening, overwhelming and exhilarating all at once. If you want to succeed, you owe it to yourself to try.

Regret is a bitter bedfellow. People are usually haunted by the things they didn't have the courage to try.

If you try your best, even if it doesn't work out you know you could have done nothing more to change the outcome.

Your Abundant Moment of **Initiative**

Begin small today.

Abundance Minded People [AMP] share their knowledge and grant people access to information, ideas, people and places that they otherwise cannot go.

Go ahead and take initiative - make a difference in the life of one person today. Do something for them that they couldn't have done themselves. Sometimes, impulses that start out as a simple gesture can end as a worldwide movement.

Absorb: Grasp the essence and the message behind the story.

Comprehend: Ask yourself how the message can apply to your life, career and relationships.

Excel: Take action. Put the insight to work.

Absorb the Passion

"Nothing is as important as passion. No matter what you want to do with your life, be passionate."

- Jon Bon Jovi

The Passion of Karoly Takacs.

In 1938, Karoly Takacs, a Sergeant in the Hungarian Army, was the top pistol shooter in the world and was widely tipped to win gold in the upcoming 1940 Olympic Games in Tokyo. Then disaster struck. In an army training session, a hand grenade exploded in his hand and blew it away. The potentially gold-winning right hand was gone and many professed that it was the end to his Olympic dream.

At that point, most people would have quit and probably spent the rest of their lives feeling sorry for themselves.

Karoly could have cursed his fate and wallowed in self-pity. But Karoly was made of sterner stuff. After a month in hospital, Takacs did the unthinkable. He decided to learn how to shoot with his left hand.

Instead of focusing on what he didn't have – a world class right shooting hand - he decided to focus on what he did have – a healthy left hand.

With incredible mental toughness, Takacs practiced secretly for months until the spring of 1939 when he showed up at the Hungarian National Pistol Shooting Championship.

The other shooters approached Takacs to give him their condolences and congratulate him on his courage to come watch them shoot.

An Abundance of Passion 41

"I didn't come to watch," he told them. "I came to compete." He competed and won.

When the Olympics were cancelled in 1940 and 1944 because of World War II, it looked like Takacs' Olympic Dream would never have a chance to become realized. But Takacs kept training and, in 1948, he qualified for the London Olympics. He competed, shooting with his left hand, won the Gold Medal and set a new world record in pistol shooting.

Four years later, Takacs won the Gold Medal again at the 1952 Helsinki Olympics.

Károly Takács was only the third known physically disabled athlete to compete in the Olympic Games after George Eyser in 1904 and Olivér Halassy in 1928.

He was also the first shooter ever to win two Olympic gold medals in the 25 metre rapid fire pistol event, both with his left hand.

Comprehend the Passion

Passion is fuelled from within and winning begins in the mind.

Skills can be acquired but it is mental toughness that brings about success. Winners know that they cannot let circumstances keep them down.

Winners in every field have a special trait that helps them become unstoppable. They recover quickly. They push themselves and find a way to succeed.

This ability allows them to survive major setbacks on the road to success.

Instead of focusing on what you cannot do, focus on what you can do.

With determination comes the passion to succeed and passion fuels fulfillment. With renewed focus comes a positive final outcome.

When you live your life with passion and a purpose to serve, your life takes on a direction of excellence and you find joy in the celebration of progress, not just perfection.

Be a river not a reservoir.
Flow with passion.
Become fulfilled by giving your all.

An Abundance of Passion

Loving what you do gives birth to passion.

Demonstrate your passion in your speech, actions, services, products and genuine relationships with other people.

Excel through Passion

1. Be present in your life.

When you are present to every moment of life, you keep your passion alive.

**Face your past without regret,
handle your present with confidence
and prepare for the future without fear.**

2. Be yourself, be authentic.

When you are sincere and do things from your heart - when you love what you do – that's when you express passion. That's when there will be an authenticity that comes through to those around you and those you work with.

3. Do your best to be your best.

Start taking action right away. Even accomplishing small things fuels passion and brings fulfillment. It is that inner satiation you feel when you are doing what you were created to do.

4. Passion makes you search for a solution not an escape.

When a challenge rears up, make the decision to dig deep inside and find a solution, a way around the roadblock.

An Abundance of Passion

5. When you get knocked down, get up quickly and take action.

Quick recovery is important because, when you recover quickly, you don't lose your momentum and your drive.

6. Our word is our worth and our worth is our word.

When we keep our word, we demonstrate our passion to fulfil responsibilities. Fulfilling promises is very important in everyday life and essential for long-term success in all areas of life.

Your Abundant Moment of **Passion**

Let your passion create quick, simple victories.

A person is fulfilled when he or she accomplishes something, great or small. Go ahead - do the one thing that you have always wanted to do. Do it without any expectation of monetary gain. Maybe you love to cook or play the guitar. Attend a cooking class, sign up for a music workshop or invite friends over for an impromptu gig. Realizing one's dreams, however small, emboldens the passion and brings a feeling of self-worth.

Even more importantly, let your passion help someone else accomplish one of his or her small successes. We all have the ability to connect with our inner glow and then express it in a way that benefits others. These small victories can uplift others and you too, in a great direction forward.

CHAPTER 5
An Abundance of

Absorb: Grasp the essence and the message behind the story.

Comprehend: Ask yourself how the message can apply to your life, career and relationships.

Excel: Take action. Put the insight to work.

Absorb the Activity

"I saw the angel in the marble and carved until I set him free."

- Michelangelo

Brian and Jan, co-founders of WhatsApp.

Brian Acton and Jan Koum, both former employees of Yahoo, founded WhatsApp Inc. in 2009. By January 2014, this globally popular mobile messaging app surpassed 700 million users. The following month, the cofounders inked a deal with Facebook and sold their company for $19 billion. The acquisition cost was 13 times Facebook's entire 2013 net income and almost 2.5 times Facebook's 2013 gross revenue.

In 1992, when Koum was 16, he and his mother emigrated from Ukraine to Mountain View, California. She worked as a babysitter and Jan swept floors in a grocery store to make ends meet. When his mother was diagnosed with cancer, they lived off her disability allowance.

By 18, he had taught himself computer networking by purchasing manuals from a used bookstore and returning them when he was done. He enrolled at San Jose State University and moonlighted at Ernst & Young as a security tester. In 1997, he was working at Yahoo when he found himself sitting across a desk from Brian Acton, a 44-year-old Yahoo employee.

Over the next nine years, the pair watched Yahoo go through multiple ups and downs. Acton invested in the dotcom boom and lost millions in the 2000 bust.

In September 2007, Koum and Acton finally left Yahoo. Both applied to work at Facebook but were turned down.

It was the age of the Apps boom and Koum had an idea for an app that would have statuses next to individual names. The statuses would show if you were on a call, your battery was low or you were at the gym.

Koum almost immediately chose the name WhatsApp because it sounded like 'what's up', and a week later, on his birthday, Feb. 24, 2009, he incorporated WhatsApp Inc. in California. Koum and Acton developed WhatsApp in coffee shops and at their homes. It took just a few years before the app was worth billions of dollars. Today, it has over 450 million active users per month with many million photo uploads and voice messages sent every day.

As a young immigrant, Koum and his mother had to rely on food stamps. In a poignant tribute to his humble past, he chose to sign the deal with Facebook at the same welfare office in Mountain View where he used to queue up to get food stamps.

Comprehend the Activity

Irrelevancy in the tech business world can happen remarkably fast, especially in companies where industry leaders soon lost lustre. All companies risk becoming irrelevant. New technologies, customer behaviour patterns, regulations, inventions and innovations constantly challenge old success formulas while changing communication requirements alter the use and impact of things like images, photos, charts and text.

In such a highly interconnected, fast-paced, globally competitive marketplace, Facebook and WhatsApp were not immune to changing market trends. That's why Facebook's acquisition keeps both brands relevant in mobile platforms and imaging.

Facebook and WhatsApp have given a lesson in an alternative approach.

1. Recognize the market shift. Accept it. If there is a better solution, rush toward it rather than ignoring it.

2. Bring these new solutions into the company. Embrace integration and expend efforts to find synergy.

The Abundance-Minded Person (AMP)
has a desire to push his frontiers,
to reach higher levels of influence
and to go beyond what has been
previously accomplished.

When it comes to performing a routine activity, there's really not much difference between an ordinary person and an extraordinary person. What separates them is that little something, that extra effort or idea that stands out and surpasses the usual expectations.

An Abundance of Activity   55

How to unleash and open the floodgates to unlimited Abundance.
1. A little extra effort.

The person on top of the mountain didn't just land there. He or she made an effort to get there. Only those who dare to take risks and courageously take initiative can reach extraordinary heights.

2. A little extra time.

Abundance Minded People, the high achievers, develop daily. Personal growth does not happen in a single moment but takes place over a long, slow process. If you aspire to accomplish something great, be prepared to devote enough time to it. Stay calm and patient as nothing worthwhile happens quickly.

3. A little extra help.

The Abundance Minded Person can appear solely responsible for his or her own success but you can be certain he or she received incredible support to make it to the top. Even the extraordinary person needs good opportunities and sound advice in order to succeed. Without these aids, a person's potential cannot be reached.

4. A little extra realism.

To be extraordinary, AMPs can neither run from reality nor shut their eyes to it. They have to see their situation as it actually is and not as they wish it would be. Realism provides the concrete foundation on which an AMP can pursue his or her dreams.

5. A little extra change.

In order to improve their lives, people must change themselves as well as their circumstances. They cannot simply change their job or relationship or place of residence in order to better their lives. To be productive and become successful, they must continually improve themselves by upgrading their abilities and leadership skills.

6. A little extra thinking.

As Earl Nightingale said, "You are and you become what you think about." Your mind will give you returns based on what you put into it. If you wish to make withdrawals, make huge deposits first.

7. A little extra attitude.

Motivation determines what you do and ability determines what you are capable of doing. But it is your attitude that determines how well you do it. Whenever you see someone performing with excellence, you can be sure they have a great attitude.

8. A little extra planning.

Thinking through what's truly important and planning how to invest your time and resources are what matter most. It is the planning that allows you to be more efficient and effective.

Excel through Activity

Make your activity meaningful.

How can you make a contribution in your life, whether at home, at work or in your community? What keeps you on top of your game? Can you share it with others?

Giving abundantly makes the world a better place.

It can impact future generations for the better. Those who come after us will have only what we leave them. We are the stewards of this world and, as such, we are called upon to leave it better than we found it, even if in a seemingly small way.

Giving is an act of responsibility.

Purposefully making a contribution to the better good of all breaks the grip of selfishness that can be inherent in us. It keeps us focused on the big picture and on the long-term impact of our actions.

Give excellence.

Strive to be your best every day in all that you do. As you work toward excellence for yourself, you inspire excellence in others.

Serve as a role model for your children, your friends and your colleagues. You can leave your mark by raising the standards and actions of everyone around you.

An Abundance of Activity   59

Give encouragement.

Adopt a voice and attitude that offers hope and encouragement. Lift people up by your very presence and your interest in others. Do you have a teacher or mentor who encouraged and motivated you? Become that person for others. Be a positive voice in a world of negativity.

Give purpose.

What are your strengths and skills? You may have some that you take for granted but that others see as quite valuable. Use your strengths and talents for a higher purpose. If you write, create something useful or inspirational. If you are a good listener, keep on open ear for those who need encouragement and a place to speak their minds.

Give love.

Think about the people who love you. What kind of impact have they made on your life? Now think of those you love. Let them know how you feel through your words and actions.

Love is the most valuable contribution you can ever make. Express and receive it, openly, abundantly and joyfully.

Give abundantly and your actions will be felt way beyond your expectations.

Your Abundant Moment of **Activity**

Make your life about something bigger than yourself.

Every word you speak and every action you take can be a contribution for a higher purpose. Bring your awareness to this concept and begin to see your life as a platform for touching the world in a positive way.

Take a small step today. Proactively find three avenues to apply your talents and skills in ways that serve others and bring joy, humour, beauty and love into the world.

Absorb: Grasp the essence and the message behind the story.

Comprehend: Ask yourself how the message can apply to your life, career and relationships.

Excel: Take action. Put the insight to work.

Absorb the Value

"Try not to become a man of success, but rather try to become a man of value."

- Albert Einstein

Ben Kaufman, The value in the Quirky idea. Founder and CEO of Quirky.com

"We started the company to make invention accessible," says Kaufman. "People come to our site, submit their ideas and the best new ideas make their way all the way to retail shelves and we do all the heavy lifting in between."

Have you ever had a great idea for an invention but weren't sure how to make it a reality? That's what Quirky.com is all about. This New York based start-up is literally the stuff dreams are made of.

Kaufman was in high school in 2005 when he created Mophie, a company that makes add-ons for the iPhone. Shortly after Mophie won "Best of Show" at MacWorld 2006, Ben discovered his passion for involving people around the world in the development of new consumer products.

The rapid growth of Mophie led to its acquisition in August of 2007, which allowed Ben to focus his efforts on bringing his idea of 'social product development' to the next level.

After two years of research and development on the unique technology platform that became the foundation of his future work, Ben publicly launched Quirky in June of 2009. Today Quirky has already put hundreds of products on store shelves from Target to Walgreens, Bed Bath & Beyond and Amazon.com.

"I wanted to build a business where the best product ideas in the world actually got out there into the world," Kaufman says. "So we started the company to make sure that no matter what disciplines you know or don't know, you're augmented by both an expert team and a community that can make sure your product idea gets out there."

Community is key to Quirky. Every idea submitted online is screened and voted on by Quirky employees and an active group of online users during weekly meetings that are streamed from its New York headquarters.

Once a product gets the green light, the online community submits ideas about everything from the colour of the product to the name and tagline. If your idea is selected, you become a part owner of the project and receive royalties for every unit sold.

"Everyone asks what makes a successful product," Kaufman says. "I think the biggest commonality is that it solves a problem everybody has. "

Quirky soon made it to the Forbes list of "America's 100 most promising companies" and Ben then made it to the top of Inc. Magazine's "Top entrepreneurs in the country under the age of 30".

Quirky now has more than 417 products in development and a community of 1083K inventors.

There are thousands of ideas submitted to Quirky every week. Deciding which of these ideas are the best is in everyone's hands. You can vote on the ones you love and help Quirky's inventors bring the best ideas to life.

Every Thursday, a group of industry experts, friends and community members get together at Quirky New York headquarters and debate the best ideas that have been submitted that week. Before going home, they've chosen the next products that will be worked on.

In the end, the world has access to one more invention that has a chance to make the world a better place.

And as his company improves, Kaufman has his sights set on some lofty goals. "In five years, I would like Quirky to be the best consumer product company in the world," he says. "In ten years I would like us to build the spaceship that brings us to Mars."

Comprehend the Value

The value of a global idea.

Quirky adds value to the world community because anybody can submit an idea. It doesn't matter if it's a little doodle, a crazy chemical formula, or a "wouldn't it be cool if...". Quirky makes it possible to share an idea - the first step toward bringing an idea to life.

Your progress is proportionate to your perceived value.

Each one of us is where we are today as a result of the value someone placed on our lives or as a result of the value we placed on other people's lives.

Since decisions powerfully shape our lives,
it is our choice of values
that put our choices in context
and simplify our decision-making.

Also, with the right values, we opt for the right decisions more consistently if we know what values we hold and the value we place on making the right choices .

An Abundance of Value

The consequences of a major decision can influence us for years or even a lifetime.

Each day we face a specific context in which we must exercise judgment in making the right call. Of course, not all decisions are equal. Some major decisions, particularly those about our personal values, give direction to all of the other choices we make.

Excel through Value

How to create lasting value:
1. Individual value.

We always get the greatest return by focusing our effort to grow in those areas where our natural ability (what we do well) intersects with our natural affinity (what we love to do).

Decide to grow every day by developing your strengths. Being intentional about personal growth offers great value in return. Take the time to study and practice and gather advice constantly.

2. Adding value.

Remember the universal axiom: The more we give, the more we receive.

Decide to add value to others before expecting value from them.

> **There are two basic rules to attract the best results in your life.**
> > **Whatever it is that you want, you have to want it more for someone else.**
> > > **And anything you want, can and will be yours**
> > > > **as long as you're not the only one who would benefit from it.**

And so, when you make a purposeful habit of helping others reach their goals, they will eventually help you attain your own aims.

3. Sharing value.

Pouring yourself and your inherent talents into the betterment of others is like channeling water into a river; what you add is carried onward and can provide enrichment several miles downstream.

On life's journey, you'll always go faster alone but you will inevitably go farther in partnership with others.

4. Multiplying value.

When we give with no expectation of return, we are acknowledging the Abundance of the universe.

We are demonstrating faith that the good we do will benefit others close to us and the world at large – and that good things will come back to us.

The circle is never broken. The more you give, the more you receive and the more you can give back.

The best reason for adding value to anyone, anywhere is the basic joy of making a difference in other people's lives. This concept creates an Abundance Minded Universe.

Because you are happy for the success of others and enjoy meeting like-minded people, Abundance Mindedness will allow you to get what you want in all areas of your life and put you on the road to greater success.

Your Abundant Moment of **Value**

Exercise your faith in Abundance. Add a little value today.

Abundance Minded People know that giving with no expectation of return is a great way to feed Abundance. They understand that solid, lasting, mutually beneficial relationships are at the core of generating Abundance.

Reach out to someone today. Build them up either through a kind word or positive action. Strengthen an existing relationship or build a new one by building people first.

Absorb: Grasp the essence and the message behind the story.

Comprehend: Ask yourself how the message can apply to your life, career and relationships.

Excel: Take action. Put the insight to work.

Absorb the Trust

"I've learned that people will forget what you said, people will forget what you did, but people will never forget how you made them feel."

– Maya Angelou

Maya Angelou, the Global Renaissance Woman.

A teacher, activist, artist and human being. She was a warrior for equality, tolerance and peace.

Maya Angelou was born Marguerite Annie Johnson on April 4, 1928. She was an African-American author, poet, dancer, actress and singer. She published seven autobiographies, three books of essays along with several books of poetry and was credited with a list of plays, movies and television shows spanning over more than 50 years.

Angelou is best known for her autobiographies, which focus on her childhood and early adult experiences. Her autobiography *I Know Why the Caged Bird Sings* tells of her life up to the age of 17 and brought her international recognition and acclaim. It made her the longest-running African-American author on the New York Times bestseller list for paperback non-fiction.

When she died on May 28, 2014 at the age of 86, she had become one of the world's greatest and most beloved spiritual voices and is remembered for all she did that was good and meaningful.

She accomplished so much, touched so many and did it all with integrity and honesty. She stayed true to herself and, in doing so, created a stronger impact than she could have done otherwise.

Her life experiences coloured her outlook, as they do with most people, but she learned to be reflective at a young age.

She was the epitome of powerful goodness. Her ability to describe a beautiful way of living, of being forgiving and kind, and of telling stories truthfully are some of the qualities that made her beloved and her books' bestsellers.

Comprehend the Trust

Trust is the purest form of love and respect.

Trust is the natural expression of unconditional love and respect. All lasting relationships are built on trust, dependability, honesty and accountability.

Man thrives on relationships but only those built on trust can have the solid foundations required for them to last.

Building trust is like constructing a house. It takes time and it must be done piece by piece, with patience. Abundant Mentality People develop that same trust with people. People rely on them and trust their integrity completely.

Trust abounds and flows limitlessly when we follow a set of basic standards. When we conduct ourselves in line with these standards, we build durable relationships with strong foundations.

These are the principles employed by Abundance Minded People who have proven to be successful in life.

a. Positivity.

People with Abundance Mindedness are a source of positive energy. They are intrinsically helpful and genuinely concerned for other people's welfare. They seek positive solutions and strive to inspire and reassure. They avoid personal criticism and pessimistic thinking, looking instead for ways to gain consensus and help people to work together efficiently and effectively as a team.

An Abundance of Trust

b. Honesty.

Abundance Minded People treat people as they themselves want to be treated. They are ethical and honest. Effort and reliability form the foundation of their success. They inspire trust.

c. Inspiration.

Abundance Minded People are truly inspiring relationships masters. They are people who communicate clearly and, by doing so, motivate those around them to give their best all the time. They inspire people around them to give their best by offering support and latitude for others to pursue their dreams and become the best they can possibly be as well.

Excel through Trust

How you can ensure a limitless flow of trust.
1. Always keep your word.

Being a person of your word makes you reliable so that others can count on you to honour your promises and commitments. Keeping your word means living consistently so that your actions align with your professed values. Finally, keeping your word demands integrity, acting in a forthright and truthful manner so that others can be sure that you sincerely mean what you say.

2. Unconditional love and respect.

People instinctively know inauthenticity when they see it and they will withhold trust from someone when they sense that person does not respect them. Teach yourself to see the best in people and communicate that you value them and that you appreciate their contributions.

3. Truth and trust go hand in hand.

Speak the truth even if it is uncomfortable. We trust people who help us discover the truth. The truth may not always be pleasant but people will trust you more when they know that you have risked their discomfort and anger to stay honest and true. They will become accustomed to being challenged by you occasionally.

If you help people confront reality and make positive changes as a result, their trust in you will grow. In every relationship, communication and action ensure that you keep your word, demonstrate unconditional love and respect for others and courageously speak the truth in love.

An Abundance of Trust

4. Own your failures.

An obvious way to build and maintain trust is by owning our failures. See each act of ownership - not as a display of weakness - but rather as an opportunity to build trust.

Owning our mistakes builds upon and maintains the trust that we are working hard to establish with other people. We cannot be honest with others about their shortcomings and then refuse to face our own.

5. Empathy.

Trust is built upon concrete and conscious empathy. Empathy is built on the foundation of speaking the truth. But there must be humanity in the speaking of truth. Always communicate with good manners and without malice.

6. Self-trust.

People who can trust others are those that trust themselves first. If you're not honest with yourself, you're not capable of honesty with others.

Trust is ensured with:
Honesty, when our words and deeds are in alignment.
Transparency, when we are not hiding.
Accountability, when our motives are sincere.

Your Abundant Moment of **Trust**

Trust is never given but earned.

It must be earned and retained and that requires constant effort, but it is worth it.

Affirm your trust in your people by doing what's right. When people share their opinion, really listen with intent. And always perform your actions with excellence giving it your very best. When people see you embracing these values, they'll appreciate your integrity and it'll go a long way towards building trust.

Absorb: Grasp the essence and the message behind the story.

Comprehend: Ask yourself how the message can apply to your life, career and relationships.

Excel: Take action. Put the insight to work.

Absorb the Kindness

"The difference between what we do and what we are capable of doing would suffice to solve most of the world's problems."

- Gandhi

Craig Kielburger and the kindness of Free the Children. Free the Children brings kindness back to our daily lives.

Free The Children is an international charity, youth movement and educational partner who's credo is that all children in the world should be free to achieve their fullest potential.

In 1995, when Craig Kielburger was 12 years old, he read an article about the murder of a 12-year-old Pakistani boy named Iqbal Masih, a former child factory worker who had spoken out against child labour.

That same year, Kielburger established a charitable organization he called *Free the Children*. Its purpose was to raise awareness in North America about child labour and to encourage other children to get involved in the issue. In an attempt to learn more about child labour, Kielburger then travelled to South Asia to meet child labourers and hear their stories first-hand. It was on that trip that Kielburger captured the attention of the North American media.

In 1999, at the age of 16, Craig Kielburger wrote *Free the Children*, a book detailing his journey to South Asia and the founding of his charity. In 2007, his book was re-released through *Me to We Books*, *Free the Children*'s social enterprise partner organization which offers summer leadership '*Take Action*' camps and international volunteer trips for youth. Through school or youth groups, young

An Abundance of Kindness

93

people can travel overseas to take part in development projects for which they have helped raise funds.

Free the Children works with schools and families in developed countries "to educate, engage and empower young people as agents of change." Through their holistic and sustainable development model, *"Adopt a Village"*, they work to remove barriers to education and to empower communities to break the cycle of poverty.

They do so through their overarching program called *We Act*, a year-long service-learning program which provides youth, educators and schools with access to free resources, support materials and enhanced program components like a team of Youth Programming Coordinators who mentor school and community youth groups. They also provide curriculum resources for elementary, middle and high school classrooms; online resources; service campaigns; action kits; professional development sessions for teachers and motivational speaking tours and workshops.

Every year, *We Act* launches a day of inspirational sessions which features notable speakers such as Al Gore, and Elie Wiesel as well as performers such as Demi Lovato, Justin Bieber, Jennifer Hudson and Nelly Furtado. Attended by thousands of students, tickets are not purchased but given instead to students who earn their tickets through service in a local or global cause.

Today, *Free the Children* has built more than 650 schools and schoolrooms in developing regions worldwide and has established offices in Toronto, Montreal, Vancouver, London, England and Palo Alto, California.

Comprehend the Kindness

Nurture a sincere desire to help others.

**Think about the people who are close to you
and the everyday challenges they face,
the responsibilities they carry
and the resources and the help
they need.**

Show that you care enough and do something thoughtful to demonstrate that you value them.

Even small action creates a ripple effect.

A 2010 study by researchers at Harvard University and the University of California provided the first real evidence that kindness is contagious. They found that recipients of kind gestures tend to "pay it forward" by helping other people who are unrelated to the original gesture and so launching a cascade of caring behaviour.

The best and easiest way to make an impact with kindness is to stop and really look around.

Once you have really allowed your eyes to see what is happening to people around you, try to identify their practical and social needs. But don't stop there. Then purposely choose one of those needs and take a step to meet it.

An Abundance of Kindness

You will be doing more than helping other
people.

And a more recent study out of York University in Toronto says
performing small acts of kindness every day for just one week can
considerably increase our happiness.

Excel through Kindness

There is always room for more kindness in the world and many ways to make a difference.

1. Send out one tweet or WhatsApp message a day.

Compliment someone in hopes of bringing them a smile.

2. Create a stack of handmade Thank You cards.

You could say things like: 'Thank you for your patience", "Thank you for your smile", "Thank you for going above and beyond" and other sayings that fit the circumstances of your relationships.

3. Keep your eyes and ears open as you go about your day. Look for any opportunity to make someone's day easier. It can even be as simple as straightening that blown-over garbage can, helping an elder person cross the street or as courageous as buying a homeless person a nutritious meal or giving a lift to a stranger on a snowy day who looks too frail to make it on his or her own.

4. Try to see beyond yourself.

When you consciously seek to understand other people's challenges, you can understand your own challenges better.

An Abundance of Kindness

Seek to understand the diverse perspectives of others,
see the needs of people around you,
and realize that fulfilment means sowing seeds that benefit others.

5. Grow beyond yourself.

Push yourself beyond your present capacities and aim to learn from others who have accomplished what you aspire to. Seek out experts and admirable leaders and ask them for advice and mentorship on how to help in your community.

6. Invest yourselves in other people's development.

We have to give to others before we can expect to win their support. Reaching new levels of influence requires living in a way that makes a difference in the lives of others. That is how our own lives become more meaningful.

Your Abundant Moment of **Kindness**

Sow a small seed of kindness. Do for others that they can't do for themselves.

Today, offer an opportunity to someone that they can't reach on their own.

Introduce someone you know to people they can't know on their own.

Share an idea or two that will broaden their scope.

One selfless act of kindness, one small trickle today is all it takes to unleash a torrent of Abundance tomorrow.

CHAPTER 9
An Abundance of GRATITUDE

Absorb: Grasp the essence and the message behind the story.

Comprehend: Ask yourself how the message can apply to your life, career and relationships.

Excel: Take action. Put the insight to work.

Absorb the Gratitude

"It is not happiness that makes us grateful, but gratefulness that makes us happy."

- Brother David Steindl-Rast

The amazing gratitude of Batman - the blind man who taught himself to see. Daniel Kish, President of World Access for the Blind.

Daniel Kish has been blind since he was a year old. Yet he lives a full, active life as any sighted person would.

Kish was born with an aggressive form of cancer called retinoblastoma which attacks the retina. To save his life, both of his eyes were removed by the time he was 13 months old. Since his infancy, Kish, who is now over 44, has been adapting to his profound blindness in remarkable ways.

Ever since his eyes were removed, he has made clicking noises with his tongue to understand his environment. Daniel Kish navigates his surroundings by listening to the echoes as his clicks bounce off surfaces. He has trained his ears to understand the echoes.

He wasn't aware he was doing it as a child, just as sighted people don't consciously teach themselves to see. This is called echolocation, the same technique that bats rely on to fly in the dark. Beluga whales and dolphins also use this technique.

When he was growing up, his parents supported his clicking and encouraged him to have a 'normal' childhood. His friends all rode bikes and he also wanted to, so he taught himself by riding next to a wall and clicking to stay in a straight line. Gradually,

An Abundance of Gratitude   **105**

he was able to ride to school and to friends' houses on his own using echolocation.

He has given a name to what he does – he calls it 'FlashSonar'. "Anyone could do it, sighted or blind. It's not rocket science" says Kish.

Kish is so accomplished at echolocation that he is able to pedal his mountain bike through heavy traffic and on precipitous dirt trails. He climbs trees. He camps by himself, deep in the wilderness. He has lived for weeks at a time in a tiny cabin, a two-mile hike from the nearest road. He travels around the globe. He is a skilled cook, an avid swimmer and a fluid dance partner. Essentially, Kish can see.

Despite a lack of support from every mainstream blind organization in America, Kish is now seeking nothing less than a profound reordering of the way the world views blind people - and the way blind people view the world.

Kish is the first totally blind person to be a legally Certified Orientation and Mobility Specialist (COMS) and hold a National Blindness Professional Certification (NOMC). He also holds Masters' Degrees in Developmental Psychology and Special Education.

Kish is also President of *World Access for the Blind*, a non-profit organization founded in 2000 to facilitate "the self-directed achievement of people with all forms of blindness" and increase public awareness of their strengths and capabilities. Kish and his organization have taught echolocation to at least 500 blind children worldwide.

Daniel Kish has a high sense of appreciation for life and a deep gratitude for the other senses and exceptional skills he possesses. He has always had high expectations from life and is a living example of how gratitude and high expectations can empower everyone to accomplish amazing things in life.

Comprehend the Gratitude

There is ample research to prove gratitude works. According to a study conducted by Dr. Robert Emmons, a University of California Psychology Professor, "the practice of gratitude helps us to cope better with stress, gives us greater health and increases positive feelings such as hope, peace and happiness."

Gratitude lets you live with purpose.

Gratitude means living your life with a purpose to serve and direct your life with excellence, giving your best effort in all you do.

In return, accomplishment leads to gratitude as it increases our sense of personal worth.

Gratitude leads to fulfillment.

Grateful people are positive, happy individuals who lift others up. They may not have everything in life but are grateful for what they do have.

They make the best of each day and share what they have with others.

Gratitude strengthens relationships.

When we feel gratitude,
we can allow ourselves to recognize that
others wish us well.
In turn, we feel loved and cared for.

An Abundance of Gratitude

Logically, we could say that gratitude implies humility and an acceptance that we could not be who we are or where we are in life without the support and contributions of others.

Abundance Minded People inspire abundantly.

History is full of examples of great men and women whose ability to give created massive amounts of value for the people and the world around them. They were able to harness their creative resources not only for their own benefit but in ways that allowed them to inspire others by the things and ideas they invented, built, pioneered or discovered.

Before we seek Abundance, we must learn to give Abundance.

That is the only way we can experience gratitude. Our generosity to others, by our words and actions, will fill their lives with joy and happiness. Their fulfillment will bring fulfillment to us.

Excel with Gratitude

1. Wake up to gratitude each morning.

Every day we wake, we have another chance at this wonderful experience called life.

> Gratitude means being present to every
> moment of life.
>> Appreciating the bright colours and beautiful
>> aroma of flowers,
>>> taking in the deep blue sky, dancing to the
>>> rhythm of life,
>>>> and listening to the laughter
>>>> of children.

All these inspire gratitude which we can find everywhere when we are present in our lives and able to appreciate it fully.

2. Take simple grateful steps.

Each day, consciously go through the motions of gratitude in order to trigger positive outcomes. Simple grateful actions like smiling, saying thank you and writing letters of gratitude can work miracles.

3. Focus on your haves, not your have-nots.

Instead of focusing on what isn't working in your life, focus on the things that are. You will soon notice your negative way of thinking will begin to shift. A positive outlook will allow you to experience the happiness that is waiting for you.

An Abundance of Gratitude   **109**

4. It just makes so much sense.

As seen through Daniel Kish's eyes, the human body is a miraculous piece of construction. Each of our senses - touch, sight, smell, taste and hearing - can give us an appreciation of what an incredible miracle it is to be alive and accomplish great things.

5. Spread it generously.

Share Abundance with everyone - talk health, happiness and prosperity to every person you meet. Be enthusiastic about the success of others. Wear a cheerful countenance and give every person you meet a warm smile. Positivity and gratefulness, even love, directed to those who matter or complete strangers, has a constructive and healthful effect.

Your Abundant Moment of **Gratitude**

Set aside one minute today.

In fact start today and set one minute aside every day - to recall one moment of gratitude associated with everyday events or the value someone added to your life. And make sure to thank him or her for that.

Write a simple letter or email of gratitude to a friend, colleague, spouse, family member or some other important person in your life whom you've never properly thanked.

CHAPTER 10

An Abundance of

COURAGE

Absorb: Grasp the essence and the message behind the story.

Comprehend: Ask yourself how the message can apply to your life, career and relationships.

Excel: Take action. Put the insight to work.

Absorb the Courage

"Courage is not the absence of fear but the triumph over it. The brave man is not he who does not feel afraid but he who conquers that fear."

- Nelson Mandela

The unbelievable courage of Yi Sun-sin Korean Admiral of the 1500s.

In Korean history, which spans over five millennia, there have been many national heroes but none more heroic than Yi Sun-sin, who saved his nation from the brink of collapse during the Japanese invasion of 1592.

Admiral Yi achieved a battle record that no one in history has ever matched. Genghis Khan lost two battles out of the 20 that he fought. Napoleon Bonaparte lost four battles out of 23. Emperor Frederick lost four battles out of 12 and Hannibal lost one battle out of five.

Yi was never defeated in all of his 23 battles. Overcoming formidable odds in terms of the number of ships and troops he had, he led his navy to victory in every engagement he fought during seven years of war with the Japanese, losing only two ships of his own.

As soon as he became a naval commander, even though it was not yet clear that war was imminent, he took up the task of reviving and restoring the Korean Naval Force. While he accomplished unbelievable feats at sea as an Admiral, his absolute loyalty to his country and people enabled him to achieve the maritime miracle of uninterrupted victories.

An Abundance of Courage

Of Admiral Yi's 23 sea battles, the most crucial were the Battle of Hansan and the Battle of Myongnyang.

1. The Battle of Hansan.

Considered among the greatest naval engagements in history, Yi won the Battle of Hansan by means of his famous 'Crane Wing' formation and achieved a great victory by sinking and capturing 59 of the 73 Japanese ships which opposed him, thereby frustrating Hideyoshi's plan of advancing along the coast.

2. The Battle of Myongnyang.

The Battle of Myongnyang, in which Yi defeated 130 enemy ships with only 13 ships of his own, is regarded among maritime historians as nothing less than a miracle.

In the early morning of September 16th, Yi received news that a fleet of 330 Japanese ships was approaching his base on the Myongnyang River. After calling on all his captains to take the Oath of Valour, he put out to sea at the head of his fleet, ready to engage an enemy with the only 13 ships of the Korean Navy.

He arrayed the ships in *Ilja-jin* (One Line) formation and waited. Owing to the narrowness of the channel, only 130 Japanese ships were able to come in to attack and, before long, they had surrounded Admiral Yi's fleet. Outnumbered by 10 to one, the overwhelmed captains of the Korean Navy began to pull back in fear. Yi's flagship sped forward alone into the midst of the advancing enemy, fearlessly bombarding them with a constant volley of arrows and gunfire.

As the Japanese fleet enveloped the flagship, Admiral Yi's sailors lost heart. But he did not. "Though the enemy may boast of his thousand warships," he told his men, "he will not dare come near us. Have no fear! Engage the enemy with all your might".

Stirred to action by his words and his own actions, the ships of An and Kim charged the enemy line at full speed and fought desperately.

Taking advantage of the tide's new direction, the confined nature of the battleground and the cumbersome size of the enemy fleet, Yi's fleet drove the enemy into defeat. Of the 130 enemy warships that entered the Myongnyang Strait, 31 ships were sunk and more than 90 were severely damaged; none of the Korean ships were lost.

In 1598, at the age of 54, he died gloriously in his final battle at Noryang which concluded the Seven Year War. He was posthumously titled Chung Mu Gong (Duke of Loyalty and Arts of Chivalry).

Comprehend the Courage

Courage is what gives a person his or her ability to continuously act with confidence in any situation whether it is out of necessity or desire.

Courage in both its physical and moral forms is required for a person to become the best version of himself or herself.

Courage is not some unattainable trait that can only be achieved by a small number of special people. Anyone can become courageous. First, you have to make the choice to be bold. Then, all it takes is time and training. You can't erase fear, but you can override it.

It takes courage to recognize and be comfortable with yourself.

Accept who you are and live it.
Don't worry about fitting in.
Concentrate on what you want to become
- someone authentic, honest
and trustworthy.

Courage can only come by actively seeking to build it. You build courage by taking action. Often, of course, that means taking action towards those very things that you are most fearful of.

An Abundance of Courage

Excel though Courage

1. Get comfortable with feelings of fear.

Getting comfortable with feelings of fear is the first step to becoming courageous. Once you accept it, you can overcome fear by stepping out of your comfort zone until discomfort begins to seem comfortable. Courageous people are simply those who are not afraid to step out of their comfort zone.

2. Boldness starts in the mind.

Always believe in your abilities and imagine yourself as a courageous person. See yourself as bold and you will behave boldly. It is confidence that breeds greater confidence.

3. Remember the good bold times.

Think of your past successes. Identify those strengths that have helped you get where you are today. Chances are that you'll succeed again and again. Focus on what goes right and what you get right.

4. Gain specialized knowledge.

The person with facts is always stronger than the person armed only with opinion. Do the research that will help you gain specialized knowledge to destroy fear. Only by acquiring specialized training can an untrained pilot overcome his fear of flying.

5. Kill fear by acting on the very thing that causes it.

Experience erases fear. The only way to overcome your fear of something completely is to experience it. Courage is created by action. Boldness is a quality that can be honed by repeated actions to fight fear.

6. Bold moves start as small decisions.

Wishing and hoping will not make it so. If you have a big dream, break it into small steps. Taking each of those small steps will eventually lead you to a place where you can leap forward.

7. Celebrate your courage.

Each time you take any bold action, you'll make progress.

Celebrate your mistakes, failures, small wins and big victories.

It all counts and contributes to building your reserves of courage.

Your Abundant Moment of **Courage**

Identify the one thing that you have always avoided and never done before.

Identify your deepest fear and work hard to get beyond it.

Try often and you'll soon build your courage muscles to a point where you can move ahead and get where you want to go.

Bulldoze through your fears by taking immediate and bold action.

Absorb: Grasp the essence and the message behind the story.

Comprehend: Ask how you can apply this message to your life, relationships and career.

Excel: Take action. Put this insight to work.

Absorb the Integrity

"Good habits formed in youth make all the difference."

- Aristotle

David Esposito and the Integrity of The Kids' Abundant Harvest® Board Games.
Inculcating the virtues of integrity through the formative years.

When David Esposito, a combat veteran, returned home after the war he confronted a world that seemed to grow in complexity, intensity and uncertainty. Even as he witnessed a rapid pace of change in our world, our businesses, our communities and, most definitely, in our homes, he could sense that the great change brought along its own set of challenges.

According to David: "As our world has become more connected with things like the internet, smart phones and social media, today's 'online chatter' has actually caused our families to become more disconnected. We are losing the critical life skill of effective face-to-face communication. The struggles of today's families and the unique journey through adolescence in our digital world continue to be some of the most heart breaking of all of life's challenges."

David, along with his wife Tracy, founded the Harvest Time Partners Foundation, a charitable organization dedicated to developing products and services that help individuals, families and organizations with character-building opportunities worldwide.

Harvest Time Partners also created a series of conversation games called Abundant Harvest® to help families and educators open the door to more effective communication and encourage

An Abundance of Integrity   **131** decision-making based on principles such as honesty and loyalty, with the intent of reinforcing the Law of the Harvest which simply states: "You reap what you sow."

Among other things, the Kids' Abundant Harvest® Board Games create teachable moments for parents and educators, support open discussion on real-world issues, help children to develop the critically important life skill of face-to-face, authentic communication and, most importantly, reinforces the value of developing character.

The Abundant Harvest Games are designed to teach players how to make good choices based on strong moral decisions.

How it works: Each player chooses a moving piece with words such as Honesty, Courage, Love, etc inscribed on it. The player rolls the dice and when it lands on a spot, the child picks up a corresponding scenario card. The scenario is read out loud and the player tells the group how he or she would respond in that scenario. The rest of the group encourages that player and then others are welcome to share what they would have done. The challenge is to respond using some of the good, moral character traits that are listed on each person's card such as honesty, faithfulness, loyalty, strong work ethic, compassion, etc.

Each spot on the board 'pays' the player who lands on a 'good' spot with an Abundant Harvest. The first one to reach the end is the winner.

Today, these award-winning conversation games are widely being utilized in families, schools, counselling programs, and faith-based organizations worldwide.

Comprehend the Integrity

Who are you when no one is looking?

While ethics or practices are an external system of rules and laws, integrity is an internal system of principles that guides our behaviour. The rewards are intrinsic.

Personal integrity is the foundation for success.

A person who has worked hard to develop a high standard of integrity will likely transfer these principles to other areas of their life.

People of integrity are guided by a set of core principles that empowers them to behave consistently to high standards. The sum of virtues such as compassion, dependability, generosity, kindness, maturity, objectivity and respect equals integrity.

Integrity gives birth to trust.

When you hold a sturdy rope, you trust its integrity because it is well constructed with a series of shorter fibres interwoven with longer ones, all braided together with great care.

Similarly, integrity is also the effective interweaving of many virtues into reliability and honesty. When you possess these virtues, your thoughts, words and deeds will be in perfect alignment with each other, exhibiting integrity every time.

An Abundance of Integrity

The right thing to do is not always the easy thing.

It takes awareness and courage to act in that moment; to hold out for a choice that is in alignment with your stated ethics and the integrity of those involved.

Honesty and a strong self-image go hand in hand.

A person lacking self-esteem, healthy relationships and emotional stability is more prone to acting without integrity. The reverse is equally true. A person with high self-esteem, a strong support system and a balanced life will most likely act with integrity. Hence, the key to exhibiting integrity is to first develop strong self-esteem.

Excel through Integrity

Integrity is a choice rather than an obligation.

Even though sometimes influenced by upbringing and exposure, integrity can be cultivated purposefully with a strong intent. Integrity conveys a sense of wholeness and strength. When we are acting with integrity, we do what is right - even when no one is watching.

1. Be thoughtful before you take even the smallest false step.

Think before you take that first small mis-step.

If you don't compromise on the little things,
   you are less likely to go wrong on the bigger ones.
      There is nothing more valuable than the ability
         to look at yourself in the mirror with a clear conscience.

2. Be strong enough to ask yourself uncomfortable questions.

Each day, our integrity will be tested in many unpredictable ways. During these challenging times, develop the courage to ask the right question and you will know the right answer. Here is a sample list of questions to guide you in the right direction:

An Abundance of Integrity

- Do I believe this is the right thing to do?
- Am I being fair and considerate?
- Would I want others to act the same way towards me?
- Is there someone I could talk to who could help me enlarge my perspective?
- Is this the right time, intention, person, place and style?
- Could I make an adjustment in my actions that would prevent or alleviate harm?
- How will I feel about myself afterwards?

3. Demonstrate the right signs of integrity.

When you are honest with yourself and with the world around you, you will be more likely to act with integrity. This will also allow you to channel all your efforts to dealing more honestly and effectively with the challenges of your life.

- Balance your perspective with the needs of others
- Respect views that are different
- Be open to feedback
- Be humble and seek the advice of others
- Exhibit understanding and compassion
- Accept personal responsibility

4. Acting with integrity, even when no one is watching, is a sign that your efforts are being rewarded.

Your Abundant Moment of **Integrity**

Today, commit to finishing what you have been holding back.

Are there areas of your personal life where you have delayed taking action? Is there a difficult situation at work that you have been avoiding to confront? Have you chosen instead to take the easy way and not deal honestly with your feelings?

Today, take the first step towards integrity by being honest with yourself and confronting the situation. Say what you mean and do what you say you will do. Simply walk the talk.

When you take personal responsibility for your life and your decisions, the intrinsic satisfaction of having done the right thing will liberate you and make you feel proud.

Absorb: Grasp the essence and the message behind the story.

Comprehend: Ask how you can apply this message to your life, relationships and career.

Excel: Take action. Put this insight to work.

Absorb the Self-esteem

"Everything can be taken from a man but one thing: the last of human freedoms - to choose one's attitude in any given set of circumstances, to choose one's own way."

- Viktor E. Frankl

The unshakeable self-esteem of Viktor Frankl, Auschwitz Death Camp Prisoner #119104.

Viktor Frankl, Jewish neurologist, psychiatrist and Holocaust survivor, is often referred to as the ultimate prophet of hope and herald of positive psychology.

In September, 1942, Frankl was arrested in Vienna and transported to the Nazi concentration camp of Theresienstadt with his wife and parents. Three years later, when he was liberated from the dreaded Auschwitz death camp, most of his family, including his pregnant wife, had perished. But prisoner #119104, Viktor Frankl, had survived.

The years he spent in the concentration camps deeply affected his understanding of reality and the meaning of human life. In his famous book, *Man's Search for Meaning*, he tells the story of how he survived the Holocaust by finding personal meaning in the experience and how that gave him the will to live through it.

Frankl clearly saw that people with a lower self-esteem and lack of purpose died quickest in the concentration camp. He watched fellow inmates succumb to what he called "giveupitis". One day, they would simply lie in bed and refuse to get up, ignoring beatings and abuse from the guards. At that point, Frankl sadly noted, they had given up their reason for living and their death usually came within a day or two. Without purpose, they had no reason to go on.

An Abundance of Self-esteem   **143**

During his captivity in Auschwitz, he realized that the only thing his captors couldn't take from him was his state of mind. Even in the degradation and abject misery of a concentration camp, Frankl was able to exercise the most important freedom of all - the freedom to determine one's own attitude. No SS guard was able to take that away from him.

Viktor Frankl spent four years in Nazi concentration camps during World War II where he endured slave labour such as digging frozen earth with his bare hands and constant hunger, torture and the scourges of malnutrition and tetanus. He survived some of the most inhumane treatment in modern history when every moment was a test against the dehumanization by the Nazis whose aim was to take all humanity from their Jewish inmates and the threat of the annihilation of his people.

What can we learn from a man stripped of all his family, worldly possessions and dignity? After his liberation, Frankl went on to establish a new school of existential therapy called logotherapy that was based on the premise that man's underlying motivator in life is a "will to meaning," even in the most difficult of circumstances.

Frankl has shown that the greatest human triumph is achieved by the defiant human spirit, even when we are stripped to our naked existence and confronted with horrific death. His life is a testament to this kind of courageous hope and demonstrates how an Abundance of self-esteem can help us triumph over even the greatest of adversities.

Comprehend the Self-esteem

Self-esteem is simply how a person views himself and his abilities. Feeling positive about oneself helps us create a high Self-esteem. Naturally, the reverse is equally true.

Self-esteem plays a great part in how well we do in our lives.

> **Our opinion of ourselves, our abilities and our innate talents**
>> **affect our thought patterns.**
>>> **These thoughts lead to appropriate actions.**
>>>> **High self-esteem gives us the determination to succeed.**

Even today, "giveupitis" is manifest in the world. A low self-esteem can lead to a lack of motivation, energy and excitement. It can hold you back from chasing your vision and goals and keep you stuck in the ordinary. Only strong self-esteem can make you spring out of bed in the morning and generate the energy to push for what is really important even when you feel the magnet to give up.

The only way to be truly happy is to decide to be happy. It starts with you - your own perceptions of yourself, your abilities and your potential.

We hold the power to decide whether to devalue or value ourselves. We hold the key in our own minds whether we will succeed or not.

When we develop the ability to recognize and acknowledge our capabilities and our own perceptions of our value as a person, then we can succeed in any life endeavour. That ability and understanding becomes crucial when we are faced with the hard challenges that go with life.

Believing in yourself is simply part of an overall self-care strategy for wellness and contentment. Even though you can't change any of the circumstances of life, you can change the way you think and respond to the realities you are faced with.

Self-esteem can unleash your potential to turn adversities into opportunities.

Excel with Self-esteem

1. Have an optimistic attitude in your life and yourself.

Adopt a frame of mind that makes you really feel good with every passing day. This may sound clichéd - it is not the situation but your response to the situation that matters. So make sure that you have a cheerful and positive outlook about life in general and yourself in particular. Try to stay in good spirits and check the mirror often to see if you are smiling. This will make your day more enjoyable and fun.

2. Finesse your communication abilities.

The ability to communicate effectively, with good writing, speaking and listening skills, will definitely go a long way in boosting your self-esteem. Learn to speak clearly and dynamically in a polite, assertive and inspiring manner. In that way, you will be able to communicate ideas effectively in a variety of situations.

3. Hone your interpersonal skills.

Enhance your social life by developing the courage to interact with new people. Start to become more friendly and approachable and believe in the people you meet. Remember, a stranger is a friend you haven't met yet. Also attend networking events, workshops and seminars which will enable you to develop your self-confidence as well as boost your self-esteem.

4. Aspire to enhancement not perfection.

Nobody is perfect and that applies to everyone. When you plan your objectives, strive for the very best but also acknowledge the probability of lapses. If you find yourself accepting nothing but perfection, you will end up being discouraged and upset. Make it your aim to simply be better than before in whatever endeavour you choose.

5. Watch your self-talk.

The one person we speak to most of the time is ourselves. Be careful of the thoughts that cross your mind. Thoughts become words, actions and consequences very quickly. And it all starts with the life we give to them through the words we think.

Always speak powerfully *[turn to Page 157 for 18 Daily Affirmations]* and replace the sub-conscious habit of describing situations with a conscious habit of identifying solutions. Talking about challenges weakens the spirit while focusing on the triumphs gives strength.

6. Be the king/queen of comeback.

Things happen - to everyone. This means that you need to be upbeat and hopeful. Do not worsen things by brooding over all the depressing things that you are going through. Figure out a way to overcome your challenges.

We all have had experiences in which we have felt proud of ourselves. Think of those moments often and use them as guideposts to remind you what you are capable of.

7. Take care of yourself.

Eat healthy, exercise regularly, get adequate sleep and endeavour to dress well.
Grab every opportunity to improve your personality.
Read, search and research resources on personal development.
And seek out and associate with AMPs as often as possible.

Adhering to these basic steps will ensure you feel good, both within and without. It is a sure-fire way to develop your self-esteem.

In my first ACE book, *The ACE Principle*, I talk about some people who curse the darkness and some others who light a candle. Which one are you?

Your Abundant Moment of **Self-esteem**

Think about your greatest and most fulfilling moments in life.

Think about some of the tough situations when you were close to giving up. What was the spark that kept burning and got you through? What was your driving force to achieve these amazing feats?

Think about the most important people in your life. What do they mean to you and how do they inspire and motivate you?

Now write down one power statement for each that make you feel proud about who you are and what you did.

Read them out loud to yourself and keep them as reminders to inspire yourself each time you are confronted with a new challenge.

Congratulations. By creating your own set of three powerful affirmations*, you have just taken the first step towards building a strong self-esteem.

You can find more such Abundance affirmations on Page 157.

BONUS

12 Ways to Excel as an **Abundance Minded Person** - an AMP

Here are 12 quick, easy ideas that you can start implementing right away to create your own Abundance domain – summed up from everything we have learned in the previous 12 chapters.

1. Focus on the Abundance, not its lack.

Try to see the world as an abundant, providing, friendly place. Soon ideas and opportunities that hold solutions will spring to mind that will open up your world. Perhaps they have been there in the background for quite a while but when you focus, they suddenly jumps out at you. And thus, you can be receptive to a world that actually provides rather than restricts. You'll see a world that wants you to be successful and abundant rather than one that conspires against you.

2. Speak right.

Be selective with what you put into your mind. Create your own environment of Abundance. Even if it feels like you have a scarcity right now, you can turn that around by reminding yourself of all the things to appreciate in your life. Try to remember other times in your life when you have had Abundance and realize that you can recreate similar circumstances once again.

153

3. Eliminate.

Consciously move away from negative people and eliminate the negative influences that rob you of positive energy. Avoid addictive substances, negative people and unproductive pastimes if you want to attract more Abundance into your realm.

4. Appreciate.

Appreciate the simple things in your life that give you pleasure - your family, your friends, good food, your home, and the beauty of nature around you. You cannot be in a sour mood for long when you look at a tree or a lake or a bright summer sky. Make it a habit to appreciate your life a few minutes each day. Try to create a more open aura within you, one that makes it easier to focus on the Abundance.

5. Associate right.

Cultivate relationships with people that have the same goals, ideas and Abundance philosophy as you do. Be positive towards the Abundance and success of your friends, family and co-workers. Be generous with your compliments and good feelings.

6. Initiate actions that support your feelings of Abundance.

Act in ways that promote your feelings of Abundance and success. Act on those passionate emotions as if the Abundance and success you seek is already here.

7. Align thoughts, words and actions.

Align your desire for Abundance with your beliefs about your ability and worthiness. In an attitude of allowing, all resistance in the form of thoughts of negativity or doubt is replaced with simply knowing that you and your universe of access are one and the same. Picture the Abundance you desire freely flowing directly to you.

8. Be present in the moment.

Use your present moments to activate thoughts that are in harmony with creativity, kindness, love, beauty, expansion, Abundance and peaceful receptivity. Notice this moment, right now. Don't wallow in thoughts of hopelessness that comprise your belief system.

9. Spread it generously.

Keep the flow of abundant energy moving. Be generous with your time and energy. Don't stop the flow of abundant energy by hoarding or owning what you receive. Keep it moving.

10. Remember that your prosperity and success will benefit others.

The supply of Abundance is unlimited. The more you partake of the universal generosity, the more you'll have to share with others. Use your prosperity in the service of others and for causes greater than yourself. When your candle lights a hundred others, your eminence does not diminish but the world becomes a brighter place.

11. Pay it forward.

Selflessness - the sincere concern for the well being of others – is the secret to instant empowerment. Believe in yourself and enjoy the fact that you have the ability to make a difference. Make the words, "How can I help you?" part of your everyday vocabulary. Start today, choose to pay it forward.

12. Celebrate and reward yourself.

This is the fun part of building self-esteem: rewarding yourself! Think of all of the hard work you do every day, and find a reason to reward yourself with something nice.

Irrespective of what's happening in your life, list your positive attributes and reflect on them daily. Remember that each item on the list, however insignificant it may seem, is a reason that you are worthy of respect and love. Acknowledge negative feelings and reframe your response with positive reminders of your self-worth.

ABUNDANCE AFFIRMATIONS
Print this and repeat it **every day**.

I am surrounded by Abundance. I always have what I need when I need it.

My life is mine to create. My life is full of Abundance.

By appreciating what I already have, I manifest more Abundance.

I am grateful for every single moment in my life.

My world is filled with an Abundance of wealth, health and happiness.

I am consistently presented with new opportunities and success.

I passionately live a life of Abundance and success.

I am known for my positive energy and abundant lifestyle.

I manifest Abundance with my unique gifts and talents.

I produce financial Abundance doing what I love.

I make meaningful contributions to society.

I am surrounded by people who are eager to contribute to my Abundance.

I abundantly seek inspiration and mentorship from other successful people.

I listen to others with patience, compassion and understanding.

I communicate clearly, gracefully and professionally.

I create the exact lifestyle I want to live with enthusiasm.

I choose happiness, success and Abundance in my life.

I live an abundant life. All of my dreams are coming true right now!

REFERENCES

The book would not have come about without the fantastic men and women who have demonstrated and continue to demonstrate how to live an Abundant life and change the world for the better through their examples. It has been a pleasure to explore their personalities, their work and their contributions.

Each of their lives has been a huge inspiration. I have tried my best to pay homage to their accomplishments. All the reference sources have been listed below.

Chapter 1:

http://kelseyserwa.com/

http://en.wikipedia.org/wiki/Kelsey_Serwa

Chapter 2:

http://en.wikipedia.org/wiki/George_de_Mestral

http://inventors.about.com/library/weekly/aa091297.htm

Chapter 3:

https://pencilsofpromise.org/

http://en.wikipedia.org/wiki/Pencils_of_Promise

http://en.wikipedia.org/wiki/Adam_Braun

Chapter 4:

http://en.wikipedia.org/wiki/K%C3%A1roly_Tak%C3%A1cs

http://www.britannica.com/EBchecked/topic/581102/
Karoly-Takacs

Chapter 5:

http://en.wikipedia.org/wiki/WhatsApp

http://en.wikipedia.org/wiki/Brian_Acton

http://en.wikipedia.org/wiki/Jan_Koum

http://www.facebook.com

https://www.whatsapp.com/

Chapter 6:

http://en.wikipedia.org/wiki/Quirky

https://www.quirky.com

Chapter 7:

http://www.mayaangelou.com/

http://en.wikipedia.org/wiki/Maya_Angelou

http://www.biography.com/people/maya-angelou-9185388

Chapter 8:

http://en.wikipedia.org/wiki/Free_the_Children

http://www.freethechildren.com/

http://en.wikipedia.org/wiki/Craig_Kielburger

Chapter 9:

http://en.wikipedia.org/wiki/Daniel_Kish

http://www.worldaccessfortheblind.org/

Chapter 10:

http://en.wikipedia.org/wiki/Yi_Sun-sin

http://www.britannica.com/EBchecked/topic/653203/Yi-Sun-shin

Chapter 11:

http://www.harvesttimepartners.com/

http://www.harvesttimepartners.com/wp-content/uploads/
Game-Article.pdf

http://www.harvesttimepartners.com/david-esposito/

Chapter 12:

http://en.wikipedia.org/wiki/Viktor_Frankl

http://www.viktorfrankl.org/e/lifeandwork.html

OTHER BOOKS IN THE ACE SERIES

The ACE Principle

One of life's best gifts is the knowledge that, whether a person is six or sixty-five, he can change. You too can make better choices, develop worthwhile habits and create new opportunities.

Small act. Big impact. Little bits of knowledge applied consistently can create big results. If you are inspired to take action and raise the bar in even one area of your life, this book would have truly served its purpose.

Absorb. Comprehend. Excel… ACE your way to success.

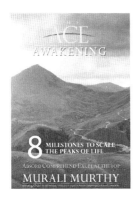

The ACE Awakening

How do you stay grounded? Climb a mountain.

The author shares his experience of trekking across one the most inhospitable terrains in India and overcoming extreme challenges to successfully climb five perilous peaks.

Using his experience of reaching the top of the mountain as a metaphor to the challenges in life we all face, Murali Murthy brings you the 8 Milestones that will help you on the journey to reaching the Pinnacle of Excellence in your own life.

Get Your Copy of *The ACE Principle* and *The ACE Awakening* from Friesen Press – www.FriesenPress.com.

When you purchase any ACE book you will be helping support Autism Charities. Isn't that wonderful – helping kids in need. Proceeds from Sales go to supporting

SOUTH ASIAN AUTISM
AWARENESS CENTRE

www.SAAAC.org

Printed in Canada